OUTSIDER

OUTSIDER

Poems and a Poet at One with Nature

DOMINIQUE MILLER

Copyright © 2025 by Dominique Miller

All rights reserved. This book or any portion thereof may not be reproduced or used in any manner whatsoever without the express written permission of the publisher except for the use of brief quotations in a book review.

Printed in the United States of America

First Printing, 2025

979-8-218-67131-0

Editor and Designer: Tonia Jenny www.toniajenny.com

Published by Dominique Miller
authordominiquemiller@gmail.com

www.dominiquemiller.com

LEAVE A TRACE IN LIFE.
DON'T LEAVE ONE IN NATURE.
RESPECT BOTH.

THUIS

O, warme westenwind
til mij zachtjes op.
Breng me naar huis
alwaar tulpen
in lage landen
geduldig wachten
op mijn terugkeer.

Hun bloemblaadjes
geopend als armen,
geven mij
een warm welkom.
Onze harten kloppen
in heldere lentekleuren,
onze woorden bloeien
teder
in de moedertaal.

*To my country, and to the loved ones who I left behind.
Seasons return, and so will I.*

All at our own pace, and with our own characteristics.

I will always love to get out into nature, and to be surrounded by those who are patiently waiting for my return.

DEDICATION

HOME

Oh warm westerly wind,
lift me up, gently.
Carry me home
to where tulips
in low lands
patiently wait
for my return.

Their petals,
opened like arms,
warmly welcoming me.
Our hearts beat
in bright spring colors,
our words bloom
tenderly
in the mother tongue.

CONTENTS

INTRODUCTION 13

1. ON THE MOVE 17

Autumn Leaf 18
New Places 19
A Bigger World 20
Horizon Line 21
Lone(ly) Wolf 22
The Milkweed & The Monarch 24
A Sense of Freedom 26
Windbreaker 28
River Valley 29
Natural Healing 30
Little Creek 32
Forest Bathing 33
Haiku I 37

2. DAYLIGHT & DARKNESS 39

Backyard Birds 40
Sleepless Nights 42
Calm After the Storm 43
Great Horned Owl 44
Tied Together 45
The Little Things in Life 46

Spring Returned 47
Sunrise 48
Stargazing in Daylight 50
Blinded by the Light 52
Haiku II 55

3. OUTSIDE 57

Restless Days 58
Wine Red 59
Tender Loving Care 60
Showtime 62
The Snowy Owl 63
Hide & Seek 64
Farewell Winter 65
Rain Dance 66
Outside(r) 67
Le Ballet 68
Dance Through Life 70
Carpe Diem 71
Romantic Red 72
The Wildness of the North 74
Suncatcher 76
Mesmerized 77
Haiku III 79

4. INSIDE 81

Self-Reflection 82
Unbreakable 83

Snow Angels **84**
Avalanche **86**
Fog **88**
Metaphoric Mirror **90**
Fragile **92**
Midsummer Cloudburst **94**
Depths of Loneliness **96**
White Dove **97**
Haiku IV **99**

5. COLDER DAYS **101**

Gently Kissed **102**
Lost **104**
Elements of Life **106**
   Fire **106**
   Wind **108**
   Earth **109**
   Water **111**
Hypnotized **112**
Haiku V **115**

6. BLANK PAGES **117**

Whirlwind **120**
Haiku VI **123**

(Published) Poems **125**
Acknowledgments **127**
About Dominique Miller **129**
Contact **130**

Contents

INTRODUCTION

My footsteps cover only a small part of an immense world, called Nature. One that's filled with healing wonders. Through observation and curiosity, I educate myself on every living being—flora and fauna—from the tiniest to the most grand. My observations add to my understanding of how nature connects to my past, my present and a future to come.

My Dutch voice shines through this manuscript, written in the language of the heart.

Spending time outdoors calms me, heals me and surprises me. I am grateful for my friendship with nature, because despite the feelings that come to me on any particular day we spend time together, she never disappoints me. Walking in her surroundings not only gets my feet moving but also my mind.

I often see my life reflected in nature, and I can relate to the wolf. At a certain time in life, I decided to leave my country the way a wolf decides it is time to leave his pack. The LONE WOLF may feel lonely, but he is not alone. Mother Nature keeps us both company.

The new territory that I explore these days, is situated in the Midwestern region of the United States. Its beautiful ecosystem became MY MUSE for writing.

A place where all my senses are triggered to the fullest—sight, sound, smell, taste and touch. Writing this book was a response to all these pleasant stimuli. I hope your imagination and your heart will be inspired by reading my poems.

Warmly,

Dominique Miller

1. ON THE MOVE

AUTUMN LEAF

My soul speaks . . .
    it wants to live life to the fullest
        in simplicity, in the light, and in motion.

So, I dance . . .
    dance somewhere, between earth and sky,
        like an autumn leaf.

NEW PLACES

Leaves
        follow
        the directions
        of the wind.

My intuition
        guides me
        in a direction.

Both
        bring us
        to new places.

A BIGGER WORLD

The tree without leaves.
On its bare branch
a black bird, placed
in the spotlight
by a bright shining star.

Eventually,
the leaves will return,
so will his flock-mates.

The star, a beacon in his sky.

Stars take part
of a bigger world,
one that's not visible
for the bird's eye.

It made me realize
that both of these worlds
are bigger than mine.

I walk this path in life,
and my world
reveals itself
to me, step by step.
The North Star,
my beacon.

HORIZON LINE

Cotton-ball-shaped clouds fill the sky. Some form clusters, others wander. A sheep herd in a celestial pasture. They cast their shadows upon earth, upon me. The lost sheep.

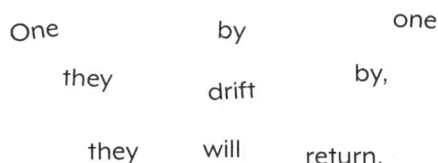

I stay here, for a little longer, not returning though.
I gaze at them, admire their shifting of shapes, their movement,
and along with them
floats my imagination.

The sky, a studio
where clouds are formed, and
daydreams created.

The birds, beautifully created too. I count them, and my blessings. I lose sight of them as they cross the horizon line to discover new things.

I'm expanding my horizon too,
in my own flow,
not pushed by any wind.

LONE(LY) WOLF

PART I – THE SON

I'm taking off
in the midst
of the night,
leaving
the love
for my pack
behind.

Imprinting
a kiss
in this soil
with every
footstep
as I go.

In silence
will I disappear,
silently
will I cry
out their names.

Your name too.

PART II – THE MOTHER

I howl
at the moon.

I call out your name
with a crackled voice.

I howl
at the moon.

I knew this day would come,
not as fast as it came,
reality sets in,
with it, the pain.

I howl
at the moon.

You will be the missing piece
in this puzzle, called *mother's heart*.
Once it was complete,
now it feels torn apart.

I howl.

THE MILKWEED
& THE MONARCH

The summer heat beats down on me,
my heart beats heavily too.
It is time for us to say goodbye.
What will remain are golden memories,
gold as the summer sun.

We mark the end of this season
with a lakeshore in silence.
I stay here, where I am rooted.
You must go; simply a visitor
like the people in this park.

You are giving me a sign
by unfolding your tiny wings
that you're ready to leave.
A gentle breeze, a farewell,
an orange dot in a bright blue sky.

You take a route southward,
one that you'd never traveled before.
Neither did your parents,
nor your grandparents.
You are doing it now
for a future generation.

That is courageous!
That is love!
I patiently wait here
for them, with open arms,
with my pinkish flowers,
ready to tell them all about you.

Note:
Monarch larvae are specialist herbivores to plants in the Milkweed family. It is generally the fourth-generation Monarch that begins migrating south to the wintering sites in central Mexico.

Source: www.monarchjointventure.org

A SENSE OF FREEDOM

In a night sky
filled with fifty
bright shining stars,
soars an eagle
across the Delaware.

He maps out the river,
his territory, our history.

He flies bravely
in the Land of the Free,
follows his instinct
as well the current
of this waterway.

Both symbols of Independence.

The eagle sees me
walking here, alone,
along the riverbank.

His shadow
covers my path,
as if he guides me
as I try to find my way
in my new land.

In this young and
spacious nation,
I find the opportunity
to spread my wings.

Like others,
I have a story
to tell, bring love
to share, and
hold a view
of this world
that isn't as sharp
as the eagle's,
it's just a different one.

The eagle's eye protects
me and my dreams,
and so will God!
His nature gives as well;
It gives me
this sense of FREEDOM.

WINDBREAKER

My skin as thick
as my windbreaker,
we both endure
storms in life.

Seams tear
Skin splits

Every stitch on the fabric,
each scar on me,
tells a story on its own.

RIVER VALLEY

Rustling leaves sing Dylan's song *"Blowin' in the Wind."*

I hum along with the leaves
while I take the next step
on this unpaved trail
that will lead me
to the top of this river valley.

This valley is a keeper of
legends and myths,
a storyteller.
I climb its bluffs though
without sharing words.

A rising sun
seems to be
my only companion,
she is my marker
in reaching the top.

The beauty of nature
makes me speechless.
However, I will return
to the river with stories
to tell.

NATURAL HEALING

Take my hand.
I guide you
through my world
of moss greens,
hardwood browns &
mystic hues of blue.
This healing place
called nature
covered in morning dew.

Inhale this dense forest.
Its fresh air
stills the mind.
Her serenity
brings peace.
It flows here
naturally
like wind
through high trees.

Look up!
Watch the birds
resting
at its tops.
You came here
as well
to rest
in the old woods
of the Midwest.

The morning sun
rises above
towering trees,
along with
the scent of pine
and pleasant melodies.

Wander here with lust.
Hug a tree.
Hum your tunes, quietly!

LITTLE CREEK

Adopt the rhythm
of this quiet place,
where water flows
and wildlife gathers.

Be here, at dawn
with the birds that bathe
and the deer that drink.

Somehow,
we slow down
at places where
water keeps running.

I came here
to reflect on life,
this little creek reflects
the morning glow,

both, simply beautiful.

FOREST BATHING

Early morning, late September,
a lightweight coat and a backpack
filled with stressful feelings.

I will take that weight off my shoulders
by visiting this healing forest,
one filled with mysterious wonders.

I greet her respectfully,
passing her entrance sign.
A blue jay greets me back,
we're both early birds.

I start a conversation
with all that surrounds me;
tall trees, tiny critters
& so much more.

We communicate in silence
and those unspoken words
are telling me a lot.

I breathe in
bright rays of sunlight
  . . . inhaling
  . . . exhaling
a warming up for my body,
a wake-up call for my soul.

Cool air blows gently,
it freshens my mind
and it colors my cheeks red
as the autumn leaves
color this forest.

My heart feels lighter
with every step I take.
Though, my legs feel heavier
as I leave miles behind me
as well as that stressful feeling.

My pace is slow
not following man-made signs,
I follow my intuition!

Now, my sneakers plow
through bright green grass
while the morning dew
kisses my white socks.
They're getting wet
by an overload of kisses.
It makes me feel fortunate
to be a nature lover.

I keep moving forward,
not ready to turn around,
even though my socks are soaking wet.
It makes me feel more grounded,
grounded in this land I'm walking on.
We both have our own stories to tell.

My giggles break the silence
as I see myself standing here
in the middle of who knows where.
Asking myself, while looking
at my wet shoes, if I'm not taking this
forest bathing too literally. Am I?

DROPS OF MORNING DEW
ARE MAGNIFYING THE WORLD
UNDER MY BARE FEET

HAIKU I

DROPS OF MORNING DEW
ARE MAGNIFYING THE WORLD
UNDER MY BARE FEET

2. DAYLIGHT & DARKNESS

BACKYARD BIRDS

By the breaking of dawn
a new song
will be sung,
like church bells
on a Sunday morning.

Awake slowly
to the fresh light
of a new day,
with chirruped tones
launched
from the arborvitaes.

Ruffle up feathers
shake up blankets,
early bird
morning routines.

Ready to take off,
just for the day
to return later
with the crescent moon
to bed or backyard.

I reflect on the day,
the reflection of wings
on my bedroom wall,
sweet tunes
my daily lullaby.

SLEEPLESS NIGHTS

A breezy wind
from the north
is clearing
the evening sky.
It's making way
for starlight,
to be admired
by those with
sleepless nights.

CALM AFTER THE STORM

The night is dark, a storm rolls through.
Its lightning brightens up my room
where I anxiously look for answers.

Heavily filled clouds hold on
to their raindrops. I hold back my tears,
a heavy weight to carry too.

The thunder, my only companion.
It shakes things up, my thoughts as well,
and both are keeping me awake tonight.

The wind does its work, being a broom,
as it sweeps things out of the way, my way,
like a cleaning in early springtime.

In this pile of mess, I didn't find every answer.
However, I found myself again, with it
my sleep.

It is the calm after the storm that finally tucks me in.

GREAT HORNED OWL

Dark
winter nights
not dark
enough
for eyes
staring
into it.

Bright eyes.

Bright stars.

Shriek tones
echoing
through
dense forest
letting all know
not to be tired
yet.

TIED TOGETHER

The rising tide
lifts the moon,
while cresting waves
mysteriously cut
through an ink-black night.

The ocean, fearless
of darkness, moves
like a thief in the night,
whereby she steals
sun, sand, and the sleep
that I couldn't find.

I will find myself to be
a witness though
to the beginning
of a new day,
as I sit here, in the arms
of moonlight,
and listen . . .

to the sound of waves
that rhythmically
echo out over the shore.

Like hands on a clock,
they push away time.

THE LITTLE THINGS IN LIFE

A silent day in nature. Her sounds muted by heavy grey skies. They took over this scenery for a week now and are slowly conquering my state of mind as well. I'm awaiting the return of the colors.

Beams of sunlight are finally finding their way through the clouds. Light always seems to be the winner in the battle for happiness. The rays are targeting me, as they are pointing a finger, to remind me to enjoy the little things in life.

That same moment, a ladybug appears. She lands on the zipper of my jacket; opens it up, and find her way towards my heart. There, she collects my negative thoughts, loads them upon her back. I can even count them. They are marking her wings with dark spots.

Her tiny legs are tickling me. It brings a smile back upon my face. Haven't seen that in days. The bug tells me to follow the light too . . . and off she goes! Left me standing here, as I'm zipping my jacket back up, realizing she was that little thing to enjoy, just as the sun reminded me to do so.

SPRING RETURNED

Spring has sprung, with enthusiasm!
Her bright rays of sunlight
opens our hearts, our windows
to let us know she kept her word
when she promised to return.

SUNRISE

The journey of the sun is infinite,
my journey in life is unpredictable.

As it stands there up in the sky, alone,
I, too, stand here alone, on this ground.

The sun became my caretaker,
her support given for free,
embracing me with warmth
to melt my hardened heart.

She became the one
to teach me about life,
now I'm facing the light
and the truth about myself.

She took me out of the shade,
gave me a new place to grow,
encouraged me to read the stars
to find my way back home.

She told me to breathe slowly
even when the clouds are passing by,
that clear skies will return
as I had to clear my mind.

She taught me as well
about those who will give me doubt
on the darkening days
when she will not be around.

She showed me how to love myself,
to trust the direction of the wind,
and today was that day
that we both rose again.

STARGAZING IN DAYLIGHT

Eyes
as blue as the sky
on a subzero day
in February.

They twinkle,
like sun-kissed snow.

I gaze into them
to read the soul,
to count the stars.

Uncountable ones
reflected in pupils
as dark as the night.

        Feeling Lucky

       when I see one

     f
      a
       l
        l
         i
          n
           g

       in bright daylight.

I sigh,
and close my eyes
to prevent myself
from falling,

falling in love.

BLINDED BY THE LIGHT

The summer sun rises
               early
Her rays are stroking the curtains,
kissing the sheets.

The heat rises fast
               too fast
at both sides of this window,
I am kissing you.

Our eyes closed
                    blinded
by the light,
and by love.

EVENING STILLNESS—
SITTING ON THE BACK-DOOR STEPS
HIS HAND TOUCHES MINE

HAIKU II

EVENING STILLNESS—
SITTING ON THE BACK-DOOR STEPS
HIS HAND TOUCHES MINE

3. OUTSIDE

RESTLESS DAYS

A whispering wind tells us that summer
is ending. That ending makes us restless, restless
as the trees. They are shedding their leaves, we are
fluffing up our blankets.

Crispy leaves are covering the trails, crunching
with every footstep; the footsteps of restless animals.
They are looking for a place to hide, as the sun will be
hiding soon as well.

We all want to snuggle up, comfortable and cozy,
before autumn leaves start singing their lullabies.
A misty night is in arrival, to bring closure to our day,
while daylight is making way for dusk.

That absence of light makes us see things in black.
Black, like the coat of a bear. The bear who is ready
to lay down on top of dark soil, tucked in by
colored leaves.

When the moon rises, the temperature will drop,
in air as well as in body, and as we all fall asleep
in the arms of fall,
winter will be awakened.

WINE RED

It is time
for mother nature
to slow down.
She exhales deeply,
lets frost air
fall upon us.

Nature recovers
in colors;
in tints of apple green,
cinnamon brown,
and pumpkin orange.

It is this red wine
that makes me
slow down,
to admire
the autumn colors.
Exhaling deeply too.

TENDER LOVING CARE

A shift in seasons
is here, at our doorstep.
It is winter's turn
to knock on the door,
to leave a dent
in my mood.

Found a remedy though,
a natural one, to escape
the winter blues.

Filled my basket
with objects from nature.
All that was handcrafted
and touched
by mother Earth,
creatively touched
by me:

a tiny twig,
a pheasant feather,
papery birch bark,
and some sunburst lichen.

Found shelter and
serenity, here in my studio.
The collected tiny treasures
now placed thoughtfully,
and in sight, next to
my wooden loom.

Working on a design
for a woven blanket,
adding threads of *love*
pulling them across with *care*,
just as nature was created.

A blanket to keep me warm
on cold winter days,
when nature will be covered
in a layer of fresh snow
I will be covered in *tenderness*.

SHOWTIME

The red carpet
of fallen foliage
is rolled back up.

The show is over,
autumn pulled down
its gray drapes.

Colors faded,
nature muted,
daylight saved.

Birds migrated,
critters found shelter,
my curtains closed too.

THE SNOWY OWL

You are the first one to admire
that white blanket of fresh snow
that was thrown down over us
last night.

The snow fell in silence
so were you in your flight,
as you moved southwards
from the Arctic tundra
to warm our hearts.

You came by surprise
like the arrival
of the first snow flurries,
both are breathtaking.

Breathtaking, as the cold air
that you are soaring upon
and we are inhaling
this early morning
in December.

HIDE & SEEK

A pile of fluffy snow
covers this tallgrass prairie,
a tiny mouse as well.

She takes cover, and hides
from arctic winter winds
and the reddish-furred fox.

Both keep their bodies warm
by playing hide and seek.
Surprisingly, a plunge!
by the fox, and temperature.

FAREWELL WINTER

April battles with the seasons, now winter doesn't want to give space to spring. The sun, the mediator between warm air and frozen ground, hangs low in the horizon to cast her light across our lands.

This winter season, long and cold, seems to be exhausted, and so are we. Yet, with fatigue, it surprises us with another storm . . . or two (!) which blankets fields and flower buds in a delicate layer of virgin white snow.

Spring brings a warm front that moves in slowly, too slow for me. But my patience will be rewarded as the sun eventually uses its force. Winter will lose its grip, snow will melt to dust off the twigs and leaves, and the birds—one by one—will fill our trees.

They return with spring, in a sky wherein winter chill's & morning blues fade away. I push myself out of the door, the wind pushes away the clouds above my head, and spring explodes. She scatters, as unexpectedly as a sneeze, her colors into the meadow. The color of my mood, the brightest!

RAIN DANCE

   . . . Hip Hip

                      Drip Drip . . .

      The Robin
      The Raindrops

   . . . Hip Hip

                      Drip Drip . . .

      Tall Grass
      Small Puddles

   . . . Hip Hip

                      Drip Drip . . .

      Wet Feet
      Empty Stomach

   . . . Hip Hip

                      Drip Drip . . .

      A Rain Dance
      A Worm

   . . . Hip Hip

                      Drip Drip . . .

      The Robin
      The Raindrops

OUTSIDE(R)

A variety of bugs
admire
this midsummer day,
just as much as I do.

We all gather here
between tall green grass
and yellow dandelions.

I see bright colored ones
in different sizes,
those with unique patterns
and funny sounds.

They all swarm
around me, and look at me.
I'm definitely the OUTSIDER here!

      . . . with my bright colored socks,
          in different sizes,
            those with unique patterns.

          I whistle happy tunes, and
          twirl with them.

LE BALLET

The sky clear,
like a glass mirror.
It reflects grasses
tall and gold, and
pathways that zig zag
between open fields
and ancestral times.

A flock of cranes
greet our land with
their distinctive call
that echoes out
over this prairie.

The birds soar
elegantly
in circles,
as they slowly
descend from the sky.

Their wings push
away spring air
to the beat of
ancient drums.

Waving grasses

Stretched wings

*Bodies that bow
and leap.*

Their gestures move
as gracefully as
ballet dancers
in modern times.

A stunning sight
for the onlooker,
the observer,
this single spectator,
for me . . .

 . . . a speechless poet,

words will come to me later.

DANCE THROUGH LIFE

A deep velvet blue
evening sky
brightened up
by flashing lights.

As if the moon
had scattered
softly glowing
disco balls
into the atmosphere.

The night fills
with fireflies, and
a scent of summer blossom.

These tiny beetles
show their dancing skills
with sparkles of joy
to impress one in particular.

She looks up,
admires the twinkling sky
as she patiently waits
in tall green grass
for him . . .
 . . . to make the first move.

CARPE DIEM

An inspiring buzzin' creature
as yellow as the sun
tumbles
through this open field,
like a tiny bouncing ball.

The elongated days
of summer, more pleasant
with a gentle breeze,
that blows him softly
over wildflowers and weeds.

He emerges from deep within
the flowers of this prairie,
BEE-ing touched by petals
of those native to the Midwest,
by their beauty too.

Fills his tiny pockets
with pollen & poems
to send a message out
into this world, one filled
with words as sweet as honey.

Finds its way back home
while the sun is setting.
He plucked the day
by seizing it, and I
I plucked his flowers.

ROMANTIC RED

Another summery day in the August heat,
one of blushing summer cheeks.
Love stories created, unforgettable ones,
in the season of cherry ice cream.

Amorous feelings are hitting the buck,
as he peeks through the shrubs.
In hiding there safely, hiding his feelings too
for her, trotting in the open fields.

Its antlers shaped as the velvet branches
of the Sumac. They protect him against
the summer sun and a broken heart.

Although, his antlers are betraying him
as they appear above the tallest branches,
and red fruits are signaling the color of love.

Those fuzzy fruits are appealing for the eye,
not only for mine, for the cardinal as well.
The bird seated comfortably in the top
of that Sumac.

He isn't paying attention to the struggling buck.
He has his eyes on the love of his life, his Muse.
Confident, not hiding at all, as he chose
the highest branch to perform his serenade.

Composed his song in a pleasant melody, and
those passionate chirped tones are filling
my heart too, with tiny red sparks.

THE WILDNESS OF THE NORTH

1:26 a.m.
Wide-opened eyes stare at the ceiling.

2:10 a.m.
The moon shimmers
on a northern lake,
a desk lamp
shines its light
on my writing.

Words flow easily
from the mind to the pen
and its ink transfers
emotions onto paper.

4:32 a.m.
Waves of words
created
in the unspoiled wilderness
where I retreat.

Nighttime quietness
overpowered
by the coffee
that percolates
on the stovetop.

6:39 a.m.
The lonely call
of the loon
resonates
through a misty sunrise.

So do my words
as I read them
from the depths of the soul
out over this lake too.

We both cry.

SUNCATCHER

She warms
my body,
the surface
of this river too.
My toes
dipped into it,
as I try to catch
the summer sun
before she will
be taken away
by autumn
  . . . (too) soon.

MESMERIZED

When summer comes
copper brown waters
won't be turning
into clear blue lakes.
Gold glowing sunbeams
will be giving it
psychedelic patterns,
leaving me mesmerized
here, at the lakeshore . . .
. . . till summer ends.

—FIRST DAY OF SUMMER—
MY FEET FOLLOW MY SHADOW
INTO A COLD CREEK

HAIKU III

FIRST DAY OF SUMMER—
MY FEET FOLLOW MY SHADOW
INTO A COLD CREEK

4. INSIDE

SELF-REFLECTION

Shattered, like a broken mirror, are sheets of ice
stacked up on this lakeshore.

I feel shattered lately too.

Strolling here, with my head kept down
in search of something, in search for myself.

In this frozen water I see a reflection,
self-reflection.

I'm like these chunks of shattered ice,
a collection of a thousand pieces.

Needed all of them, in all their different shapes
and forms, some with sharp edges.

They made me the woman that I am today,
cracks included,

still beautiful.

UNBREAKABLE

ICE
forms
this frozen lake,
it cracks.
Heavy weight
is what it carries,
feeling pressure
from both sides.
Cracking though
doesn't mean
it will break . . .

      . . . just like me.

LIFE
forms me
so did my choices,
hardened by time.
At times
I crack
feel broken
carry weight
be pressured,
but I won't break
either.

SNOW ANGELS

Big clouds promise more snow,
cover nature in silence.

I'm standing here, in solitude
to watch the flurries
to face my fears.

Along with my thoughts
drifts the snow.

Banks are formed
rapidly, just like the wall
I built up around me.

As vulnerable as I am,
so are the snow angels.
Their unexpected arrival
touches my heart.

Layers of fresh snow
crumble,
my protective wall
tumbles.

Under the debris
of self-protection
do I see a glimpse
of my inner child.

I lost her
out of sight,

a while ago

but now we're losing ourselves . . .
 . . . in the simple pleasure
of making snow angels.

AVALANCHE

*"This would have been a poem about love,
. . . if I didn't throw it all away."*

Our world shook, unexpectedly.
It set things in motion, rapidly
when shaking hands buried a lie,
one lie only.

I ignored the risks
while I tried to cover it,
and like snow on a mountain side
my mess started to move,
to tumble, to glide.

I should've protected you
from an avalanche of empty words
that rolled off my tongue.

My burden heavy
like slushy snow,
that buried me even deeper
into a place where daylight
doesn't warm lost souls.

I couldn't find my way out of it,
neither did I find the courage
nor the words
to tell you the truth.
So, I waited . . .

I anxiously waited
for the sun to shine.

Her light uncovered the truth,
which broke what already was broken.
'cause melting snow turned into tears
that bled through my paper,
when I realized I threw away
more than written words.

FOG

Fog creeps
up on
a new day.
It grabs me
by the ankles,
entangles me
like lichen
strangle trees.

It holds me
down
again(st)
moistened ground,
leaving marks
in patterns
comparable to
the bruises
on my skin.

Attacked
Vulnerable
An easy target
for predators,
not those
living in the woods;

call them
guilt
fear
and
anger.

I fight
this battle often,
throwing punch
after punch
in thin air
while the sun battles
with dark clouds.

Eventually,
when the fog
surrenders
and withdraws
you will see
that I am more
than a sinful body.

METAPHORIC MIRROR

Outside, in my backyard
leaning against this tree.
A childhood friend,
we grew old together,
noticeable physically.

Its bark
carved
by time,
the same structure
visible
in the grooves
of my skin.

Adapted here
at this place
that we call HOME.
Our beauty still unnoticed
by passersby though.

Both
tucked away
in a corner,
bended,
unable
to reach
the sky.

Unspoken words
climb up this tree
as I look at it and wonder:
Who will return to nature first,
will it be this oak or me?

FRAGILE

Protected
by tall grass and
encouraged by
bright colors of
a flowering meadow
the fawn takes
its first steps.

With beautiful
hazel-brown eyes
he curiously stares
into the future,
one that I observe
more closely.

It is in this season
wherein new life
is rejoiced and
days prolong,
that I start
counting mine.

His birth
reminds me of
the delicate balance
in nature . . .

. . . as my life,
like flowers
in late summer,
deteriorate
by a lack of love
and nurturing rain.

We both
appear fragile
in tread and
in loneliness,
aware
of that thin line
that separates
life from death.

The fawn
disappears suddenly
between coneflowers
and buttercups,
I will disappear
at God's pace
once I turn the corner
on this pathway
to paradise.
                 "bye, fawn."

MIDSUMMER CLOUDBURST

I   A midsummer cloudburst
dampens this soil, and
so do my tears.

Countless puddles
around me
darken the ground
in shades of sadness.

Shades wherein
mushrooms
appear,
as suddenly as
the death.

The rain falls
on my shoulder
as it ticks away
time, my time
without you.

II   All of a sudden
my thousand
scattered teardrops
reflect a rainbow.

Its appearance
calms this storm, and
the chaos in my head.

I kick the dirt
off my shoes,
as I'm ready
to return
towards
the bright side
of life.

DEPTHS OF LONELINESS

You went
to a peaceful place,
where the wind
sleeps
when it doesn't blow.

I'm here,
catching the wind
in my face
while staring
in the depths of
loneliness.

It waters my eyes
blurs my vision,
my memories
of you though
clear
as a cloudless sky.

WHITE DOVE

My voice unheard, muted by the sound
of city life. Words echo onto concrete walls
of skyscrapers, get stuck in webs of Wi-Fi,
or get lost on one-way streets.

Words as Maybe, Possibly, and What if.
What if . . . there is more?

I open the cage of a captured dove
that pounds inside my chest.

It will set us both free.
Free of expectations, limitations, and proofs.

The white dove guides me
to a world
I believe in, one wherein
we break bread,
and drink wine.

. . . and the wine that we pass around
will be red, red as our blood,
because in this place of harmony & hope
we quench our thirst with similarities.

LIVE IN HARMONY
WITH BIRDS BEES AND BUTTERFLIES
OUR HOME MY GARDEN

HAIKU IV

LIVE IN HARMONY
WITH BIRDS BEES AND BUTTERFLIES
OUR HOME MY GARDEN

5. COLDER DAYS

GENTLY KISSED

A drizzling rain
in March
moistens
bare lawns, and
my dry winter skin.

Its drops
fall
like gentle kisses
onto
my untouched body.

Rainwater
fills
the birdbath,
and that emptiness
inside of me.

Hidden
under the surface
this hollow space,
wherein his name
echoes against
my stomach.

He left
with summer,
what remained is
a broken heart and
the bittersweet taste
of his kiss.

LOST

Beachgoers
headed home,
just like the sun
they disappeared
for the night.

It is at this time
of the day
that tides claim
the beach back,
and so do I.

Cool sand
along the shore
massages my feet,
it tickles
cherished moments
of the past.

Bittersweet ones too,
at times
they sting
like jelly fish
or broken shells.

Tonight,
the ocean's color
has similar shades
as his eyes,
those that didn't
look into mine.

*"It is your truth
that I still can't find;
your beliefs that
I still don't believe in;
and your name
that still echoes
between sand dunes
and coastline."*

I turn around

face an empty beach

and sigh . . .

Salt water
can erase
my footsteps
but it cannot
heal this wound.

ELEMENTS OF LIFE

FIRE

A fire burns within me,

an unpleasant one.

It is hot . . . hot as hell!

I mean,
how often can you die in one lifetime?

My body burns like plastic,
it pollutes
my environment,
my mind.

My heart shrinks
slowly
to feel less,

      less pain
      less sorrow
      less memories

of you.

Its heat evaporates
my tears,
it makes me unable to put out this damn fire!

Do I stop breathing
to cut off the oxygen supply?

WIND

The wind blows

      it blows   you

          further   away
 from me.

The aftermath;

I rake leaves, collect sticks, and
pick myself up. I broke
long before the storm arrived.

I poke holes in this cloudy sky
so my words will reach you, and
light will return to my world.

In the midst of yard waste and mourning
emerges the moon.

I stare at it

and wonder . . .

What does the other side of the moon look like?
Will it be any different?
Will it be as different as my life will be without you?

EARTH

Honesty, Respect, Trust, Laughter

Sorrow, Regret, Melancholy, Nostalgia

all stuffed
in a shoe box,
one that's way too small.

I want to bury it
in the backyard,
where the memories
of you remained.

Not ready
. . . to let go
 . . . to let you go
 . . . to let myself go
 . . . to let us go.

You left me

standing here
in the cold,
on my side
stands
the illusion
that you will return.

I'm digging
in frozen ground
with broken nails,
with a broken heart.

I will try it again
in springtime,
when the ground
will be saturated
by melted snow
and fallen tears.

WATER

Rough oceans cause troubled waters.
Troubled thoughts makes life rough.

I CRY

I can't push away
the waves from shore,
neither can I get a grip on life.
They both slip through my fingers.

I SCREAM

I lick my wounds, like
a wounded animal. The tears
on my lips taste salty,
salty as this ocean.

I STARE

I dry my eyes
to comb the beach
in search for signs and shells.

I pick one up
and hear the ocean whisper;

"This too shall pass."

HYPNOTIZED

Wavy thoughts are crashing
up onto this shoreline,
where I try to calm myself.

Staring at a body of water
mine feels cold,
empty, and without direction.

Me static, this water in motion
as it hits the shoreline
in a hypnotic rhythm.

Its sound is functioning
like an eraser,

erasing it all . . .

Empty beach

Clear mind

New beginnings

TEARS OF A POET
WILL NOT DRY FAST AS INK—
UNFINISHED POEMS

HAIKU V

TEARS OF A POET
WILL NOT DRY AS FAST AS INK—
UNFINISHED POEMS

6. BLANK PAGES

WHIRLWIND

Unwritten words
keep a page blank.
Unspoken words
dry out the tongue.

My thoughts though
fill my head
to the rim,
like high water
pounding
against our dikes.

Mills pump
at full speed,
so does my blood.

Sails spin,
wind swirls,
water spits.

My words
get pushed
with force
toward the ocean,
where they slowly
will be swallowed
by the horizon line.

What remains is
this thirsty feeling,
with it, my desire to write.

THE TYPEWRITER CLICKS
A KEY PRESSED BY THE CAT'S PAW
AN ERROR REMAINS

HAIKU VI

THE TYPEWRITER CLICKS
A KEY PRESSED BY THE CAT'S PAW
AN ERROR REMAINS

PUBLISHED POEMS

<u>RESTLESS DAYS</u>, 2022, *Creatopia Studio* magazine – winter edition

<u>FOREST BATHING</u>, 2023, *MN Yoga + Life* magazine – spring edition.

<u>SUNRISE</u>, 2023, *Creatopia Studio* magazine – spring edition.

<u>THE SNOWY OWL</u>, 2023, *Poet – Artist Collaboration* chapbook by Red Wing Arts, Minnesota.

<u>THE CALM AFTER THE STORM</u> and <u>SUNRISE</u>, 2023, on view during exhibition on "Caregiving, Aging, Death and Dying." NEA Big Read in the Saint Croix Valley at ArtReach Gallery, Stillwater, Minnesota.

<u>THE MILKWEED & THE MONARCH</u>, 2022 and <u>DEPTHS OF LONELINESS</u>, 2024, selected for the poetry contest by Minnesota China Friendship Garden Society, and read by the poet at two annual "Liu Ming Yuan Moon Festival" events, Saint Paul, Minnesota.

<u>LE BALLET</u>, 2024, received an honorable mention - Minnesota League of Poets annual poetry contest; category Prairies.

GRATITUDE

ACKNOWLEDGMENTS

To all who supported me in publishing this book. Thank you for the various ways in which you have been with me on this journey.

A special thank you goes out to the following individuals who read a few poems, various sections of the book, the finished manuscript, or proofread my writing: Carla Pritchett, Marie Olofsdotter, Lou Cunico, Chris Kerr and Ciska Borsboom.

I wish to thank the members of two Twin Cities-based writers groups: Women of Words & Warrior Writers for their creative expression, motivation, encouragement and laughter.

To my editor, designer and illustrator Tonia Jenny – Tonia Jenny Publishing - thank you for your professional guidance and showing me your artistic soul, without which this book would not be possible.

Lastly, I want to acknowledge Nature, for without her, my poems would have never been written.

HELLO READER!

Thank you for purchasing *OUTSIDE(R)*, my collection of poems. May your experience reading this book be as enjoyable for you as the writing process was enjoyable for me.

Please feel free to leave an honest review of the book, or share any comments/photos on social media using the hashtag #outsiderpoetry. Your feedback not only helps other readers discover the book but also supports me as an independent author. I appreciate you!

 @bynikcreations

ABOUT

DOMINIQUE MILLER

Dominique Miller was born and raised in The Netherlands. In 2018 she ended her career in the Dutch military and immigrated to the United States.

In 2023 Dominique proudly got sworn in as an American citizen. She and her husband currently live in the suburbs of Saint Paul, Minnesota.

Dominique is a member of the Minnesota chapter of Warrior Writers—a veteran-focused, nationwide, non-profit arts organization. She is also a member of Women of Words—a writers' support group in the Twin Cities, Minnesota.

Her minimalistic style in writing brings the reader back to the basics of life, and makes her work accessible for all to read.

Creating nature-inspired poems and illustrations works for her as a bandage: *"It heals wounds, and protects cherished moments in life."*

CONTACT

NEED A SPEAKER?
ORGANIZING AN AUTHOR MEET & GREET?

Dominique loves to share about her life experiences, poems, and her love for nature. She is available for speaking—in person or via Zoom—at events or private groups, including book clubs, bookstores, writing retreats, open mics and gatherings for veterans and immigrants.

Send queries regarding your needs and options to: authordominiquemiller@gmail.com

www.dominiquemiller.com

www.ingramcontent.com/pod-product-compliance
Lightning Source LLC
Chambersburg PA
CBHW052130030426
42337CB00028B/5098